Silent Killers

Buford Harbin, III

Parks Publishing & Consulting Company, LLC

ISBN-13: **978-1-7326967-2-3**

Text Compilation: J. Tate
Editing by J.D. Parks
Front Cover Design: J.D. Parks

Published by:

Parks Publishing & Consulting Company, LLC
P.O. Box 66
Olive Branch, MS 38654

Acknowledgements

I'm so thankful. All praises and glory to my personal Lord and Savior, Jesus Christ, who has been so wonderful to me. He loaned me a gift that I didn't realize I had, which was being able to write a book!

I would like to thank my partner and friend, my wife, ReShema D.S. Harbin, for supporting me through the process of writing my first of many books. Thank you for sharing me with others who need my gift. Love you, Bae!

I, also, want to thank my parents, Buford and Dorothy Harbin, for their support and for pushing me. You let me know that you believed in your baby boy!

To my wonderful, sweet, and amazing mother-in-law, Margaret Crooks, thank you for always praying and encouraging me.

To my colleagues in the gospel---you know who you are--- thank you for continuously being in my ear, saying, "Don't give up!" I thank you so much for being real friends.

I cannot leave out the special people who the Father has blessed me to serve at The Rebuild Center. Thank you for your words of encouragement, prayers, and support. Know that I love each one of you.

Now, I must acknowledge my four amazing children and my precious granddaughter: Demarcus, Lorenzo, Jazmine, Treshawn, and my G-Baby, Alana! You all are so amazing to me in your own ways, and I thank you individually for your love and support of your Dad. I love you all so much!

And one more little thing: I want to thank my publisher, Dr. Parks, for pushing me and offering encouragement. Also, I thank you for allowing me to be the first of many clients who you are about to help publish all over the world.

To my readers, please accept my sincerest gratitude, and know that I love each one of you.

Buford Harbin, III

-1-

Silent – adjective- si·lent | \sī-lənt\: Making no vocal sound, mute, withholding knowledge, or omitting mention.

Killer- noun- kill·er | \ki-lər\: One who is a murderer or assassin.

Throughout my life, I have found myself silently struggling with many things, and other than the Bible, I had no earthly resources to help me address my problems. Therefore, the purpose of this book is to help my brothers and sisters (You) with the problems or day-to-day struggles that you suffer through, things you have been holding onto for so long. Things that, like me, you have never been real with yourself about, even though you've been wrestling with them every day. What are your struggles? Maybe it's anger or bitterness. Or perhaps, you struggle with depression. Can you pinpoint them? Do you know that you're suffering? Do you know that you don't have to suffer alone? Because I see you as my brothers and sisters, I'm here to tell you that you are not alone. Even I have worked tirelessly to pull myself out of frustration and confusion. But oftentimes, we know what we are angry or confused about, but we say, "I will just take this to my grave." That's where the term *silent* comes in, because when we hold it in, we believe that we are withholding knowledge from everyone around us, but we are actually delaying our own progress and relief. That's what the *enemy* wants us to do. My brothers and sisters, the *enemy* comes in several forms: family members, so-called close friends, and all-out haters. Understand, my friend, the enemy doesn't want you and I to release the things from our childhood or adult lives that have us bound up. So that's why he wants us to remain quiet and keep it on the inside. As a result, we're walking around with heavy baggage that's full

2

of anger, bitterness, confusion, depression, destruction, laziness, and fear. So that's why I can boldly say that you and I must not be silent any longer. If you stay silent, you will begin to fill like you are dying. So, now the term *killer*, or a murderer. Check this out: the enemy wants us to be mute because when we don't open up and free ourselves, we begin to die slowly. That's exactly what the killer does. So, understand that the enemy can quickly become your killer. For example, your enemy is fear, and if you never address it, it can and will kill you. But I pray that you will be made whole today, in Jesus' name. Join me in the fight against the enemy by joining God's army. Now is the time to open up and speak. The enemy wants to murder you, but with God, you can fight and win. Open up and speak against your silent killers!

-2-

Anger- noun - an·ger | \'aŋ-gər\: Having a strong feeling or showing annoyance, or hostility. Like for instance mad, or irritated

Bitterness- noun- /'bidərnəs/: Anger and disappointment at being treated unfairly; resentment

The first silent killers we will look at are anger and

bitterness. When I was much younger; I was privileged to

have both of my parents in the home, but there was one

problem: my dad was physically present but emotionally

absent. Some of you might be saying, "Me too, brother!"

Even though I had both of my parents, my father worked

often, and I wanted more quality time with him. I must admit

to you that I was angry, and bitterness took control of me for years. I was serving others but still traveling with all that pain. Now, understand, my friend, I really carried that with me for years. I thank God he gave me the chance to get it right and that my father and I are close now. So, you may be asking, *how do I deal with my anger? How do I get over it?* One of the things we must understand is that Ephesians 4:26 reads, "Be ye angry and sin not; let not the sun go down upon your wrath." Apostle Paul is letting us know that there is nothing wrong with being angry as long as we don't fall into sin, which is when we allow bitterness to come in and begin to control us. For example, a husband is annoyed that he is not receiving the attention he desires from his wife, so he decides to look for it elsewhere. In this moment, he has allowed his bitterness to control him, and he has fallen into sin. And this is what I did for years. I was so upset with my father that I would teach others and then go home and sit in my anger and depression. I would see others being made whole, and I wanted to be made whole. The enemy that was within me had me so trapped into being angry that I found myself in sin and returning to my old sinful, self-destructive habit of promiscuity, which stemmed from my own bitterness towards my dad. Let me say this to you, I've been serving others for twenty- eight years, and it wasn't until I started The Rebuild Center that I completely obtained freedom. Now, you can judge me if you want to, but, perhaps, you feel such anger or bitterness right now. You may even feel them down the road. It's the plan of the enemy to keep you silent. HE doesn't want you to expose the pain that you may feel; now, I know you're asking, *why did he use capital letters to refer to the enemy?* Because that's what happens to most people; the enemy becomes their personal god. It completely overtakes and controls them. However, our Heavenly Father wants you to be made whole. You have to begin now and say enough is enough because according to the word of the Lord, "Who the son sets free is free indeed" (John 8:36). Confess and believe that you are set free and receive it by Faith. After you do that, you have to keep your mind renewed at all times. One of my favorite scriptures is Romans 12:1-2, which reads:

> I appeal to you therefore, brethren, and beg of you in view of all the mercies of God, to make a decisive dedication of your bodies [presenting all your members and faculties] as a living sacrifice, holy (devoted, consecrated) and well pleasing to God, which is your reasonable (Creational, intelligent) service and spiritual worship. Do not be conformed to this world (this age), [fashioned after and adapted to its external, superficial customs], but be transformed (changed) by the (entire) renewal of your mind [by its new ideals and its new attitude], so that you may prove [for yourselves] what is the good and acceptable and perfect will of God, even the things which is good and acceptable and perfect in his sight for you.

Apostle Paul is challenging you and I to do different; in other words, he is begging us to dedicate our bodies to Christ. And that means *everything*; it is very important that you devote yourself completely to Jesus. Half way is not the way, and I will be honest with you, the enemy will try his best to deceive you. Let me give you another scripture. Galatians 6:7 reads, "Be not deceived; God is not mocked: for whatsoever a man soweth, that shall he also reap." So, whatever you sow in your mind, that's what you reap. In other words, whatever you do will come back to you. But let's jump back in Romans 12:1. Paul tells us to dedicate our bodies and faculties to Christ, which means your mind, too. You feel me? My friend, it is so important that we follow through with what Paul asks us to do. It's so important that we change our thinking; each one of us has a past. Your future is greater than your past; you have to make a now-decision for yourself. And don't remain angry. It's not worth it at all. That's all the enemy wants you to do is remain in that place of bitterness. And hear me good, when you do that, you allow the enemy to have complete victory over you. Child of God, you already have victory. All you have to do is believe it and receive it. Just start walking in your victory by confessing it and responding to your confession. Because you were born to win and not lose. Everything you need is locked up inside of you, just waiting for you to unlock it and to release it on the enemy that has tried to keep you in bitterness. Remember that being angry can cause you to slip into bitterness, and all of it is a silent killer.

-3-

Confusion- noun- /kənˈfyo͞oZHən/: Unable to think clearly, or bewildered.

Have you ever been talking to someone and all of a sudden they just break out and say, "I'm so confused." You look at them and see their mouth and nose twisted in bewilderment. Misunderstanding is all in their eyes. Oftentimes, we find ourselves confused when we're having day-to-day conversations, but there are times when we are confused about our lives. We don't know which way we're going or where to turn. In 1 Corinthians 14:33, Apostle Paul tells us as he tells the Church of Corinth that: "God is not the author of confusion but of peace, as in all churches of the saints." Yes, Paul is talking to the Corinthians, but he is also talking to us; understand that you and I make up the local body of Christ. In other words, we *are* the church. You're responsible for taking care of the Church, which is yourself. So, I'm simply saying that you must stop allowing yourself to become confused. Listen to this: if our Heavenly Father is not the author of confusion, common sense tells us that the devil, or the enemy, is. So, my question to you as believers is: why do we allow ourselves to continue to think the way we do? Apostle Paul informs Corinth and us that God is continuously passing out peace. So what is peace? Peace is freedom from disturbance and quiet. So, we have power to make a decision to have freedom, or quietness over confusion. We can get peace directly from God. So, even though we may have problems in our lives; it takes us making a personal decision to have peace over confusion. I know that during times of trouble, you have all kinds of stuff that try to come against what you know to do. But we, as believers, must change the way we perceive those things that are trying to come against us. We must use our weapon, which is the Word of the Lord, against the very things that will try to interfere in our mind and relationship with God. So, you must do the following:

1. Acknowledge your confused state by simply saying, "God, I am confused right now. I don't know whether I'm coming or going."

2. Ask God to help you identify the individual or event that caused the confusion

3. Ask God to grant you authority over confusion by giving you unlimited peace.

As long as you allow the enemy to keep you in confusion, you will be lost continuously. And you and I know that is what the enemy loves to do. The devil knows if he can keep you in this place, he has you. He aims to get your mind, then control your body, and before long, he'll capture your soul.

So, you must make a bold declaration aloud, or within yourself:

With God, I'm not confused at all.

I know what to do, and I will do what I know to do.

I will not be forced into a place of confusion again, in Jesus' name.

-4-

Depression- noun- /dəˈpreSH(ə)n/: Feelings of severe despondency and dejection

Dejection- noun- /dəˈjekSH(ə)n/: A sad and depressed state; being in low spirits

Many believers fall into depression, or rejection for different reasons. Some people become depressed because of a bad relationship, a break-up, the loss of a loved one, or being fired from a job. In many cases, the term *dejection* is tied to the word rejection, as people feel that they are unwanted, unloved, or unimportant. Hence, there are so many people going through this right now. This takes place for people in the pulpit just as much as the people sitting in the last pew at the back of the church. I pray that as you read this chapter, freedom will take place in every area of your life. Here's a story from the Bible that will help you. David was a worshipper who had a close relationship with the Father. In Psalms 34:17, David writes, "The righteous cry, and the Lord Hearth, and delivereth them out of all their troubles." Now, David made a decision within himself to always worship and praise the Lord. In the early verses, he declares, "I will bless the Lord at all times, his praise shall continually be in my mouth" (Psalms 34:1). This is the same thing we have to do as believers. We have to remain gracious, just as David did. Let's look at some more of what he says. In Psalms 34:2, he says, "His soul boast in the Lord." David has complete trust in the Lord for his next move, and that's what we have to do; we have to know that in spite of our struggles, we must continue to uplift the Father. Because as we do that, it will cause us to become excited as well. My friend, even in the midst of trouble, you must continue to lift up the name of the Lord and encourage others to join in and do the same with you. Look at what David says in Psalms 34:3: "O magnify the Lord with me and let us exalt his name together." See, you have to include others. Stop trying to come out by yourself. Make sure that you have help. In other words, talk to someone who will help you to accomplish your next move. Now, your question may be: *How do I find the right person to help me?* The answer is simple: Talk to God. Simply say, "God, I'm hurting in this area. I can't do it on my own. Send me someone, a true friend, someone led by YOU and only you, God." And watch what happens. Yes, the Lord will help you, but at the same time, he has placed others on Earth to help us through difficult times in our lives. Maybe you already have people in your life. Ask yourself these questions: What kind of folks do I have around me and in my ears? Are they negative? Snobbish? And wait for God to reveal the answers.

A large reason that many of us can't even begin to talk to God about our depression is because we will not humble ourselves. We must humble ourselves long enough to even seek the Lord's help. But if you will not admit that the problem is out of your control, how do you expect God to take control? That's another thing David did, in verse three. He sought the Lord, and God heard David as well as delivered him from all his fears. So, that means the Father will come to your rescue when we make the decision to seek him. And know when you do that, he will hear you and set you free from your fears. It is very important that you have those who really want what Jesus wants. Also, when you are fighting depression you must control your words just like your thoughts. Be careful not to talk yourself out of and into things that will prolong your depression. In Psalms 34:13, David says, "Keep thy tongue from evil, and thy lips from speaking guile." In other words, your words carry weight, so don't speak against yourself. Sometimes, when you're in a place of depression, you make statements like *I can't do it* or *I quit.* I used to struggle with my past mistakes. And that's one of the top things that the enemy will continue to throw in your face. Therefore, you must change your words.

You may be a born-again believer, or a person who has accepted Jesus, and if you're reading this and you're not born again, today is your day! All you have to do is first confess like Paul says in Romans 10: 9, "If you acknowledge and confess with your lips that Jesus is Lord and in your heart believe (adhere to, trusting and rely on the truth) that God raised him which is Jesus from the dead, you will be saved." So, my friend, it is very important that you do that. Declare that Jesus is Lord of your life, that you cancel the plans of the devil, and that you wish to kick the enemy out of your life. And vow that your life now belongs to Jesus. Then, we become part of the same family; we become a part of the body of Christ. You become what David refers to as the 'righteous'. As one of God's righteous children, the Father will hear your cry, do what you are in need of, and grant you freedom from depression. That's what the text is saying, but in order to be free, you have to admit where you are. And then, and only then, can change occur. Don't delay the process of your complete transformation. Depression is real, but with God, we can and must attack it when it arises. Don't let it take over your mind, body, and soul; You can destroy it with the Word, worship, and continuous prayer. If not, believe me when I say, that it will force you into a place that's very unhealthy. So, in closing this chapter, make up your mind and come out of that dark place. Arise in your newness, which is created by the Father for you to dwell in forever. He made us a promise in His word (Joshua 1:5; Deuteronomy 31:6; 1 Peter 5:7). Speak the word and don't let go of his promise.

-5-

Laziness- noun- /ˈlāzēnəs/: unwilling to work or use energy

I have suffered from this silent killer the most. It took me so many years to write this book, and I know how badly others need to read it so they can completely break free from whatever has them bound. Let me say this to you, the talents and gifts that Father has given you are not for you; they are for others around you. Stop sitting on your 'do nothing' and begin to do something. Now is the time, and I truly believe that when you start, you will begin to walk in your purpose, but we tend to make two crucial mistakes when we come up with good ideas that can change someone's life. First, we share it with the wrong people, and secondly, we don't accept the assignment in a timely fashion due to laziness. Laziness has no place in the character of a follower of Jesus. In Proverbs 19:5, it reads: "Slothfulness casteth into deep sleep, and an idle soul shall suffer hunger". In other words, a person who knows what to do but refuses to take action, will find him/herself stuck. Perhaps you are this person, always saying what you're going to do but never actually starting. Solomon tells us that it is absolutely absurd when you don't take action. In Philippians 1:1, we learn that it's our responsibility to *begin*. It reads, "Being confident of this very thing, that he which had begun a good work in you will perform it until the day of Jesus Christ." In other words, each of us has a work to do, and we must get up and start. So what if you fall!! Get up and start over because you have a great work to do. The Father has invested too much in you, my friend. You have to rise up, refusing to stay still and do nothing. Don't allow your mind to remain idle, or in other words, seeing yourself doing great things but never acting on them. Also, stop sleeping on your gifts because in doing so, you will continuously see others flourishing in *your* gift. I'm speaking from my own experience, as I kept putting this book on hold. Eventually, I had to say, *enough is enough*. That's when I started saying, *the time is now*. I had to know and believe that God gave me this book to help people reach greatness (no arrogance intended). So, if you are ready to experience the greatness that's in you, just start your engine up. Think about Proverbs 10:4, which reads, "He becomes poor who works with a slack and idle hand. The hand of the diligent makes rich." The term *slack* is defined as 'not content or held tightly in position, loose'. In other words, you have a grip on it, but you are just barely holding on to it. I hear you asking, what is he talking about? People are dying with purpose, and you must take full advantage of your time and don't be slack. I can't stress this enough; please sir and ma'am, start now and respond to your assignment. The world needs what you have. Now let's look at the rest of this scripture. Solomon says, "The hand of the diligent makes rich." So, as you work with the skills that the father has placed in your hands, prosperity will come upon you. The new international version in this verse reads like this: "Lazy hands make for poverty, but diligent hands bring wealth". It's up to you now. What are you going to do?

You, also, have to be careful and not share what the father deposits inside of you with everyone. It's a true statement that everyone doesn't want to see you prosper. More importantly, don't allow negative thoughts to halt your movement. You got it, and you can do it. That's what the word says in Philippians 4:13, which reads, "I have strength, for all things in Christ who empowers me [I am ready for anything and equal to anything through him who infuses inner strength into me, I am self- sufficient in Christ's sufficiency]". You have to know, like Apostle Paul says, that we have what it takes, because the greater one is on the inside to help us. So here is a question, what you are you going to do with your gifts? I hope that your answer is I'm gonna start now and do what I've been assigned to do. I beg you not to remain in your lazy, idle state. You will continue to defeat yourself when you don't respond to your calling, which is to bring change to someone else's life. So, stop saying I don't know how and snap out of your feelings and rise up. Now is the time; you have answers just like I do. God is waiting on us to work with what he has loaned us before we exit this earth. In Genesis 8:22, it reads, "While the earth remaineth, seedtime and harvest, and cold and heat, and summer and winter and day and might shall not cease." So, it doesn't matter what the season is, it's about what we are doing with what we have in that season. You have a seed, and you need it to grow so that it can change lives here on earth. Each person has seeds; your seeds bring forth supernatural manifestation in your now season that you may be experiencing right now. So, I close out this chapter and say, use what the Father has given you. And remember that it's not for you; it's for someone else. If you get up and water your gift, it will produce and multiply all over the place, north, south, east and west for the Kingdom of God. Break that laziness and get up and start somewhere; others will connect with you and help you with what you've been created to do. Arise!!

-6-

Scared- adjective- /skerd/: fearful, frightened, afraid, nervous, and panicky

So many times in life we find ourselves being scared. If we're driving down the road and lightning strikes, we say, "Oh, let me get home!" If we're in our home and all of the lights go out, we yell, "Where are the candles?!" If we call our sister or brother's phone multiple times and never receive an answer, we say, "I hope everything's okay." These are all understandable examples of fear. But where is your true confidence and faith? There are times when we know what to do and have the tools to complete the task, but we allow fear to grip our minds as well as our hearts, and all we hear is *I can't do it*. That's the trick of the enemy, to make you fearful and keep you from moving into your destiny. Perhaps you've heard this acronym before: Fear stands for (F)alse (E)vidence (A)ppearing (R)eal! In other words, you believe that you have proof or true reason to remain still, but in actuality, it is just fear operating in you. I've learned this in my twenty-eight years of doing kingdom work. As long as you allow fear to hold you, you will remain frustrated with yourself. And you'll stay in that place called *wish I could've, would've, should've did*. I understand it, but you're not a kid; you have the power of the Holy Spirit on the inside of you. So, arise, my brother and sister, and go forth in your assignment with power in Jesus' name. Psalms 34:4 reads: "I sought the Lord, and he heard me, and delivered me from all my fears." Now, understand that David said he sought the Lord, which means he began to seek after the heart as well as the ways of the Lord. And when he did that, the heart of our savior Jesus was moved immediately. After that, David was delivered from all his fears. In order to

27

break that spirit of fear, you must begin to speak the word and believe what the word of the Lord says. My friend, understand that fear is a mind thing, and you have to train your thoughts. You have to make your mind up that you're not going to live in fear. 1 Peter 5:7 reads, "Casting the whole of your care [all your anxieties all your worries, all your concerns, once and for all] on him, for he cares for you affectionately and cares about you watchfully." As believers, we should be living a life of freedom. But we allow ourselves to slip or fall back into the enemy's camp of being scared. First thing we must do is *cast*, or truly give our mess to the one who can handle it. But what we tend to do is give it to God and then turn right back around and take it away from Him. We make statements like, *I hope the Lord will do it for me*. Where is that true confidence? Here is a good example. You enter a room, looking for a place to sit. You see a chair, so you stroll over and plop down onto the chair. You take a chance by trusting the chair. But for some reason, we, as believers, have trouble trusting the Father to do what his word says. Then, we have moments that resemble anxiety attacks. Anxiety refers to "distress or uneasiness of mind caused by fear or danger or misfortune". So, now we allow the enemy of stress to come on us as well as in our minds. We also let fear grip us and make us hide like a scary cat in the corner or under the bed. But nope, you need to be free in your mind as well as your heart. So many people have tormented themselves with their past mistakes. The Bible tells us that we have power over that punk devil. So, in the name of Jesus, we curse the spirit that has tormented you for years and that has pushed you into becoming afraid. We command you to be free in every area of your life today and forever. Now, scream out loud, I'm FREE in Jesus' name! For the word of the Lord says in Isaiah 43:19, "Behold, I will do a new thing; now it shall spring forth; shall ye not know it? I will even make a way in the wilderness, and rivers in the desert." The Father promises that He will make paths and plans for us, but if we want Him to work on our behalf, we have to allow Him to take full control of how we see and think. He will make a way, even in your wilderness, or your confused state-of-mind. No one can make you move forward into your new but you. So once again, What are you going to do? Are you gonna remain in fear or are you gonna walk in freedom? The only way you can move forward into your newness is to make yourself available to the Father. Matthew 6:33 says, "But seek aim at and strive after first of all His kingdom and his righteousness his way of doing and being right, and then all these things taken together will be given to you." It's all about your mindset. My friend, it's so important that you press your way into his presence so you will know his ways, so you can deal with life's many issues. The presence of the Lord gives us access to his Kingdom. Real talk, don't be scared to step into your new; it's the will of the Lord for you to experience all he has for you. When you do, the Holy Spirit will show you how to walk and not be afraid.

So now, the choice is yours. Either you can remain in that stuck place called fear, or you can come to the place where all of your needs are met in every area of your life, spiritually, physically, mentally, financially, and emotionally! Make your new decision to live in this brand new place just for you.

-7-

Cool- noun- /kool/: Calmness or composure

So many times we lose our cool from day-to-day. And it's the enemy's goal to make you and I lose our cool when we don't see what we want to accomplish. You can't allow your enemy or the devil to make you lose your cool in the process of you moving forward in your life. When I say your enemy or the devil I'm referring to your issues or whatever is coming against you at this moment. Let's look at Matthew 17: 14-20:

> When they were come to the multitude, there came to him a certain man, kneeling down to him, and saying, 'Lord have mercy mercy on my son: for he is lunatic,

and sore vexed: for of times he falleth into the fire, and off into the water'. I brought him to thy disciples, and they could not cure him. Then Jesus answered and said, 'O faithless and perverse generation, how long shall I be with you? Bring him hither to me.' And Jesus rebuked the devil, and he departed out of him and the child was cured from that very hour. Then came the disciples to Jesus apart, and said, 'Why could not we cast him out?' And Jesus said unto them, 'Because of your unbelief; for verily I say unto you, if ye have faith as a grain of mustard seed, ye shall say unto this mountain, remove hence to yonder place; and it shall remove and nothing shall be impossible unto you.'

In this part of the text, Jesus has already trained his boys, or the disciples, but they couldn't fulfill this assignment because they didn't have faith. In this moment, they feel defeated and begin to lose their cool. You may be wondering, *how did they lose their cool?* Because they allowed the devil to make them lose their belief at that moment. But understand that the disciples aren't the only ones losing their cool. There is a son who is absolutely crazy and needs to be made whole. And that's the way a lot of us are. We begin to have moments where we just shoot off, like saying the wrong stuff, having the wrong thoughts, or acting out of character. That's the enemy's job to push you into that place of losing your cool. See, it's easy to believe in yourself and the God you serve when you're with the teacher and other students. But when you're alone, the challenge comes; the enemy tries his best to make you doubt and lose your cool. This is why you must remain in God's presence. When you spend time in his presence, the Word, and prayer, you, then, make deposits in the spirit, just like you make bank deposits. When you do that you can make a withdrawal from your account; it is the same way in the Spirit. Every time you rest in His presence, you automatically make a deposit. So,

34

that simply means that you can make a withdrawal. And this is how you make a withdrawal: In Romans 4:17, God tells Abraham: "As it is written, I have made thee a father of many nations before him whom he believed, even God, who quickened the dead, and calleth those things which be not as though they were." First, you must understand the authority that you have. It's the same that Abraham had, but your faith has to come alive in full force. You have to release faith and not lose your cool in the midst of whatever tries to come your way in the process. That's why I have said so many times in this book that you have to be in his presence.

For you to see the power of God operating in every area of your life, first, you have to believe in what you ask for. Abraham had the God-kind-of-faith. And we need that kind of faith in everything we do here on earth. When we act with the God-kind-of-faith, we're able to see and do the supernatural. Let me tell you what the supernatural is. It's the sudden and immediate results in your life. Those results only take place when we begin to speak like the Apostle Paul said in the text: "Calleth those things which are not as though they were" (Romans 4:17). So, Paul says we have to open up our mouths and begin to speak it into existence. A closed mouth doesn't get fed; results come with action. However, we have to be in place to hear His directions, and the way to hear is to get into his presence. When you do that, the Father will speak. When the father speaks, know that you can't be afraid to obey. You may ask, *why would I be afraid to obey?* Because obeying the Father causes you to be alone at times. And if you're not used to that, it can become tough. The father is ready for you to step all the way up without losing your cool. Now step out on faith and don't be like the disciples who couldn't cure that young man because of their uncertainty. As you do that, remember what Apostle Paul says in Philippians 4:19, "My God will liberally supply (fill to the full) your every need according to his riches in glory in Christ Jesus." Just know that you will not go without; I know it may look rough sometimes, but I know that help will show up. Don't lose your cool in the process and start questioning God's power because that's the plan of the enemy; his agenda is to keep you low. Speak the word, and the promises of the Lord will show up just when you least expect it. My friend, I beg you not to lose your cool.

-8-

Destroy- verb- /dəˈstroi/: Put an end to the existence of something by damaging or attacking it.

Up until this point, we have discussed silent killers such as anger, bitterness, fear, depression, laziness, and losing your cool. All of these things can lead to the destruction of your mind, body, and soul. However, with God, we have the power and the authority to destroy silent killers before they destroy us. But we must possess a mindset to do so; no one can force you to do it. In Exodus 23:24, it reads: "Thou shalt not bow down to their gods, nor serve them, nor do after their works; but thou shalt utterly overthrow them and break down their images." You must destroy each of the silent killers, one by one. They have no authority over you anymore because you're a born-again believer, and believers have so much power on the inside of us. Don't give in to those small gods because if you do, you not only give them life, but you will begin to serve them. You will become a victim to your own laziness. Can you imagine laziness leading your life? You must throw them out of your life. They aren't anything but images that want to direct you into the wrong places in your life. In Joshua 1:3, he says, "Every place that the sole of your foot shall tread upon, that have I given unto you, as I said unto Moses." The same power that God granted to Joshua can be planted in you, but you have to start to tread on it and not let it tread you down. Joshua 1:5 reads, "There shall not any man be able to stand before thee all the days of thy life; as I was with Moses, so I will be with thee; I will not fail thee nor forsake thee." Nothing can control you when you are part of God's family; you have to know in your heart and mind that the Father is with you always. He will never let you do anything or go anywhere by yourself. That's what the Lord was saying to Joshua. Joshua 1:6 reads, "Be strong and of good courage for unto this people shalt thou divide for and inheritance the land, which I swear unto their fathers to give them." You must understand your purpose is not for you, but it is to help others fulfill theirs. You have to be strong and know that the strength of God is all in you, but you have to know as well believe within yourself. There is so much the Father has for you that I can't stress it enough. Remember, my brother and sister, you must do your part and let it go, or in other words, destroy it. Isaiah 54:17 says it best for us:

> But no weapon that is formed against you shall prosper, and every tongue that shall rise against you in judgement you shall show to be in the wrong, this [peace, righteousness, security, triumph over opposition] in the heritage of the servants of the Lord [those in whom the ideal servant of the Lord is reproduced]; this is the righteousness or the

vindication which they obtain from me [this is that which I impart to them as their justification], says the Lord.

So, all the stuff that is rising against you from your past, or even now, will not stand against you. Once again, I can't stress it enough to you, my friend; you have to use your faith. That means we have to completely rely and trust what His word says on our behalf. Negative thoughts will come to your mind, and I know people are always going to talk about you. Remember, that's the plan of the wicked, but it's okay. You will survive. That's what Isaiah the prophet teaches us. Make sure you destroy everything that is trying to stop you or make you freeze up. Shout it aloud:

I WILL destroy it all!

Declaration

I am a believer, and signs do follow me.

I will put on the whole armor of God. I will put on the helmet of salvation and the breast plate of righteousness. My loins will be girded in truth. I will equip myself with the shield of faith and the sword of the spirit. (Ephesians 6:12-17).

I cast out demons (Mark 16:16-18).

I submit to God, resist the devil, and he must flee from me (James 4:7).

I have overcome the wicked one (I John 2:14).

I am redeemed from the curse (Galatians 3:13).

I am a new creature in Christ (2 Corinthians 5:17).

I am the righteousness of God through Christ (Romans 3:22).

I am more than a conqueror (Romans 8: 37).

I am believer and not a doubter (Mark 11: 23).

Therefore, I declare that I have complete victory in every area of my life in Jesus' Name.

Amen.

CPSIA information can be obtained
at www.ICGtesting.com
Printed in the USA
LVHW080216181119
637653LV00016B/469/P

9 781732 696723